Always Arising

seeking solace in an isolated world

meg grasmick

Paperback ISBN: 978-1-950685-64-6
Hardcover ISBN: 978-1-950685-66-0
Ebook ISBN: 978-1-950685-65-3

Contents

Preface

I started this book when I was navigating a tough life transition. I had just moved from sleepy Santa Barbara to sleepless New York City. I became a regular at The Bean in Union Square where I'd wait for my six-dollar cappuccino, ☕ scouring the hipster haven for a place to sit, and pull meaning from the cognitive dissonance I carried down the avenues and streets into that space.

I faced new challenges shedding my old life and reinventing myself in New York. It's a city that teaches some of the harshest lessons before you learn how to adapt and become the strongest version of yourself. And if you didn't get a little tougher, did you really live in NYC?

My motivation for writing this is to turn the pain of the past into something that lives on the page. It's also my way of transforming uncertainty about the future into an encouragement for those who experience something—anything—congruent. The human experience is nothing if not iterative and unitive.

Above all, this book is a call to action for those seeking fulfillment in the "future," whenever that is—but more on that later. I'll admit we're going to go down some rabbit holes, but stick with me.

Our lives are full of occasions when we reap the physiological rewards of getting what we want, either by luck, coincidence, or hard work. We're not chasing things; we're chasing the feeling we get when we attain them. We repeatedly act on the fallacy that the "one thing" we're seeking will satisfy us and that's it; but, whatever it is, there's no end in sight because it takes on a thousand manifestations.

We habitually long to "arrive" at some better destination or chapter in life, but arriving is both an unattainable and imaginary goal. Life is not about arriving. We can never have the ultimate authority over whether we get where we want. But we *can* redirect our focus from the tantalizing cycle of wishing. We can interrupt the story we tell ourselves by recognizing that we, in fact, are the ones telling it.

Arriving is a false narrative, but the idea of arising is full of promise. It describes both the surfacing of our thoughts and a battle cry for our lives. As our thoughts arise and ascend, so should we. Arising in life means so many things—coming into being, making ourselves known, overcoming adversity, moving up, and reaching an enlightened state.

We habitually long to "arrive" at some better destination or chapter in life, but arriving is both an unattainable and imaginary goal. Life is not about arriving.

Living in the spirit of this word is so much healthier than plowing on linearly towards arrival, which doesn't exist. If we are always arising, we are both becoming and overcoming.

I am so glad to meet you on your journey. 

Thank you for meeting me on mine.

💖🤍💖 TYSM 💖🤍💖

You Are Always on the Right Path

A friend of mine once told me, "You are always on the right path." When he first spoke this truth, I didn't understand if at all. At the time, I was going through heartbreak and distress and had never felt so lost.

As a defense mechanism, I built a wall around the aimlessness I felt because the idea of a "right path" didn't align with what I was experiencing. I refused to let even a glimmer of hope break down the fortress I had built around my heart. How could my current path lead to anything but more pain?

As the weeks inched by, slowly and painfully, I couldn't get the words out of my head. I knew that if I was going to move on, I had to embrace them wholeheartedly.

So I sat with the idea as I tried my best to reframe the harmful narrative that was ruling over my life.

I couldn't see that I was on the right path because a voice in my head insisted I was lost. It told me I had no idea where I was going and I didn't know how to read a map. I believed it until I came to realize the truth: All of that doubt was just noise. A journey doesn't begin with knowing everything that is to come, but I needed to trust myself as I figured out where I was going.

I came to realize I needed a spirit of faith, not hopelessness. So I threw back the bittersweet taste of acceptance and made room for something new, knowing it would be a spoonful of healing for my desperate soul. 🥄🥰 I needed to stand up to the indecision and self-doubt that was taking over my mind, body, and spirit. Look the beast in the eyes.

A journey doesn't begin with knowing everything that is to come, but I needed to trust myself as I figured out where I was going.

So I embraced hope in small doses and began the hard work of challenging my obsession with destination. While it wasn't easy, it became the most important personal goal of my year; living in the moment transformed into a practice, where I was forced to draw upon reservoirs of faith buried deep within that I never knew I had.

I came to accept that I had been on the right path all along. I learned that a major life change is just a natural stepping-stone to something equally beautiful, and a special chapter of life isn't devalued or diminished just because it ends.

As I was processing these thoughts, my "right path" friend invited me on a day trip to a sacred place. I knew it was exactly what I needed. In that garden under a canopy, I felt the sensation of being cared for by the universe. I listened to my friend share his own story of heartbreak, demonstrating empathy with each anecdotal gem.

I deeply cherish the gift of this experience and the unexpected kindness that softens my memory of a challenging time. My right path ally was instrumental in helping me close a chapter and embark on the healing journey. I borrowed the faith of my friend and others in my life until it was my own.

Some lessons need to be learned directly to be fully understood. Even though the growth was hard, now that I'm on the other end of it, I know for certain it was worthwhile. I learned to be a woman with faith in the evolving present rather than a girl ruled by anxiety about the future and regret for the past. I stopped doubting everything I did and started to appreciate everything I'd overcome.

I still feel the warmth and relief from the support I experienced during that time. ❤️ I couldn't see it then, but through that simple message, my friend gave me the gift of self-compassion. So if no one's told you before . . .

You, yes you, are *always* on the right path.

Darkness only exists in isolation, so lean on those that light your way and have some faith. 🌃 🙌

A love letter to my younger self

Baby beluga 🐳
You will swim the ocean once again
Again and again and again
Like a pin, dancing and twisting
Until you fall and change direction
for the millionth time today
The path you're on does not
promise lasting joy or safety
But please trust it will lead you home

Don't be hypnotized by the
things around you
Poppies, sirens, what have you . . .
Choose the purer forms of magic

Wear your joy with shameless sincerity
Lastingly childlike
As you tell the world
I'm proud of who I am
Watch all the ways I can show you
Like a toddler displays her art
Like a teenager her iron will
Like a young adult the
extraordinary ways
She's growing into herself

Your life is flooded with time
And it will build your
resilience if you let it
As you learn to get up
More quickly and gracefully
with every unexpected fall.

You Don't Write Your Story— You Tell It

Believing that you're on the right path will give you confidence in yourself and your journey, but it won't change the fact that you can't control where the road will lead. Your life is not only a path, it's a story—and one that you no doubt want to see unfold in a very specific way. So what reasonable amount of control can you assert over the story of your life?

You are a co-collaborator. The universe is the playwright, and you are the limited first-person narrator. The plot and events are written by a greater power, but you tell yourself the story of their significance and how they happened. The ability to take control over your narrative and frame your own experience is born through discernment and discipline.

Every event and circumstance that arises is an opportunity for growth, as long as you are willing to make it one. If you frame events in a productive way, it's not too hard to find something in them that is worthwhile. That is the beauty of being a curious observer and a thoughtful narrator.

Part of the freedom in telling your own story is the opportunity to create meaning rather than search for it. Instead of being a "meaning analyst," train yourself to become a "meaning creator." This will equip you with the tools you need to enrich your life all on your own.

You don't choose the events of your story, but there would be no excitement without the mystery. The universe has penned you an epic masterpiece that is full of beauty and possibility; you just have to believe it is working in your favor. The story won't be perfect, but it will be great. And you have your whole life to learn how to tell it.

Instead of being a "meaning analyst," train yourself to become a "meaning creator."

You can make sure your script is the best play ever written, simply by taking charge and bringing it to life.

In the days when I could meet a stranger

Ears popping under the East River

Feet shaking like the glass

windows of the L train

The intercom is rough, and

the tiles come too fast

My heart stops where the

train should have

I step down from the platform

and am lost again

Somehow I land where

we'd agreed to meet

My cortisol tells me to say

no thank you to the coffee

Your dog was wary of me,

but he came anyway

And on my first walking tour of
Brooklyn led by a stranger,
I learned to create the meaning
I was searching for.

Is Happiness the End Goal?

Taking on the role of the curious observer in life keeps us grounded and gives us permission to enjoy, or at least accept, our story as it plays out. The ultimate distraction from this mindful approach is our pesky obsession with happiness.

Our culture charged us with the mission to chase happiness when we were too young to know it was selling a myth. The road map to getting us there was rife with errors and, in the end, it didn't deliver on the happiness promise at all. Worse, it didn't care enough to send the messages we really needed to hear. Our culture failed us by never teaching us how to be whole.

As kids, we were not only targeted with ads in magazines, but with ideas and ideals. Wide-eyed and impressionable, we kept coming back to make sure we measured up. Through media and entertainment, society said: *Happiness is the goal. Go out and seek it by any means possible. If you don't have it, you're doing something wrong.*

Our culture failed us by never teaching us how to be whole.

It's hard to cut through the noise to make out the truth, but here it is 🗣—that story is woven with lies and wholly incomplete. We don't need the perfect partner, job, house, car—or *grrr* body—to be happy. We were fooled! The truth is there are people out there who have it all and are miserable.

This cultural narrative can toy with our sense of self-worth, which means we need to keep our filters intact. Instagram is brimming with curated profiles that suggest a perfect life is possible. If we asked someone we envy whether they were happy all the time, what might we learn?

The standards we hold for our lives should be immersed in reality, and our priorities should align with worthy and attainable goals.

Here's my personal truth: "I don't need to be happy all the time to lead a worthwhile life." As much as I wanted happiness to be my top priority, it came with too much baggage. I learned this the hard way. I cared about it so much, but I had to let it go. I wasn't a magician who could turn a fleeting state of mind into a constant reality. And I've never felt freer or more whole in my entire life.

Here's what I know now: I don't need to get everything I want. If I lead a mindful life full of gratitude and integrate wellness practices into my routine, I will magnify "the blissful state of okayness."

I am one in 7.594 billion people, all of whom experience the same spectrum of human emotion with all its mountains and valleys. I'm grateful to be a part of that tapestry and comforted in knowing I am not alone in this world of heartbreak. I've accepted the ebbs and flows of the human heart and decided that there are more productive ways to spend my energy than chasing something that can only be caught when I'm not looking for it.

Here are the things I cherish and look to grow:

My community. I choose to be surrounded by like-minded people with overlapping values, interests, and ambitions. I trust them to understand, inspire, and uplift me. The most rewarding part of any personal relationship is the feeling of being understood. If you have a friend who understands you, truly and deeply, cherish them forever.

My purpose. I mine for meaning in my work and flag the moments where I find it rewarding. While this is a good practice, I've realized that purpose is so much bigger than a job. So I've transitioned to *creating* meaning—whether it's in relationships, experiences, or memories.

While you will never be able to tame happiness, you can reach the blissful state of okayness and discover the magic of being well through small intentional choices that inspire purpose. By adding micro-improvements to your life, you will make good days better and bad days brighter. So take those small steps that inch you towards your goals; and if you don't feel like hitting them but do it anyway, you truly amaze me.

The difference between ideas and action is choosing to make strides today rather than idealizing tomorrow. Erase tomorrow; it doesn't exist! The moment is now, and it's yours, so take it. 💥 Guiding your life towards fulfillment in every moment is infinitely more gratifying than continually asking yourself whether or not you're happy.

Guiding your life towards fulfillment in every moment is infinitely more gratifying than continually asking yourself whether or not you're happy.

Harness your inner power and pay attention to the messages that add to your life. Ignore baseless claims about what will make you happy, especially if they're coming from an unreliable source. Choose to build yourself up to a state of wholeness where you can thrive and be well. 😌

Self-validation

Pixels stinging in my eyes
Blind me when I check my shape
Unable to locate meaning
in my reflection
I lay broken at the feet of an invention
And ask if I'm enough this time

The thing traces me with a chalk outline
But I blink and see it all rush back
In the mirror my perfect
pieces smile back.

You Can't Be Whole Again If You Never Break

Wholeness is the goal, and happiness is something we find along the way. When we are whole again, it means we were broken but came back even stronger through the healing process. Undergoing this transformation requires us to look past others' opinions, identify what works, and dig deeper. What are the things keeping us from being happy and whole?

Gary Vaynerchuk said it best in an IGTV video: "The number one cause of unhappiness is valuing another person's opinion about yourself above your own." If you find yourself affected by this, identify the fallacy. What do you believe about those people that makes them more qualified than you to make that judgment call? They're no better! Do they not wake up late? Lose their temper? Have embarrassing moments they wish they could erase? Fear they might fail to reach their full potential? Your opinion about yourself stands above all the rest, so don't take to heart the criticism of imperfect people.

Creating the right conditions for happiness requires you to listen to your own voice above any other, while fostering wholeness demands that you yield to the healing process. Wholeness can't do its work in you when you look at your heart as something that needs to be fixed. This is what happens when you fixate rather than frame.

Overanalyzing negative emotional states keeps you down for the count. When you treat a broken heart like something that needs to be fixed, suffering is magnified. It's very tempting to zero in on your feelings because letting them pass without judgment takes away all your control.

Your opinion about yourself stands above all the rest, so don't take to heart the criticism of imperfect people.

When sadness comes knocking, there are two productive approaches: lean in or distract. It's best to alternate between the two to avoid getting overwhelmed on one extreme or stifled on the other. Augustus Waters from *The Fault in Our Stars* reminds us: "That's the thing about pain . . . it demands to be felt." Sadness cannot be fixed.

And yet.

Your heart beats on, fighting to deliver you through to the other side. ❤️

Cherish your growth! It's a prize. Take pride in how far you've come. At the end of self is the beginning of a new thing, and there's so much left for you to discover about your own strength and potential. When you are in the trenches of the healing process, remember that everything happens for a reason and no matter the painful event, it will shape you in ways you haven't yet begun to imagine.

Here's the silver lining: Sadness passes, pain abates, and heartbreak eventually turns to indifference. Begin picking up the pieces with hope in your heart.

When you're really going through something difficult, every time you notice the sun on your face and let it bring you peace, you take a step toward gratitude. Every time you become curious about others, you take a step toward compassion. And you will keep going until your soul is content and you can wake up and be excited to make the day into something that serves you, moves you forward, and makes you love yourself in the most authentic way possible.

I listened

Living behind my eyes
Stretched thin across a grid
I find myself in crosswalks and
avenues and crowded bars
In acrylic art that swallows my wonder
In the past, from which I still run
Looking over my shoulder
In a frowning sort of smile
When I thought I was done looking

But no matter where I am
I choose to be here
Inside the things that
make me come alive
And forget the dictates of time
I'll nod to what was when
it whispers hello

The way we did when

something was still there

Thank you for what you

said, because I listened

"Never give up on yourself."

What Are You Looking For?

Sometimes happiness and wholeness seem out of reach. We were all born with an emptiness problem and have grown up searching for ways to abate it. Hungry for human connection, one place we attempt to fill the void is social media. We intermittently embark on a search mission to find our missing pieces in a tiny screen we seem to be unable to live without.

As much as I resent the time I've wasted on social media, I'm grateful to have a tool that helps me cope with stress and connect with people. However, the struggle to be mindful with endless stimulation at my fingertips makes it hard to know when to stop.

I fully respect that some will find my point belabored, and I would agree that it's not a revelation. So how did we get so sick of talking about social media? There must be real reasons why we are all addicted, and why we're so tired of talking about how addicted we are.

What keeps us in a state of social media fatigue is the fact that we can't answer the simple question: "What am I looking for?" We can swipe for hours without knowing why.  Endless feeds put us in a perpetual state of searching, while all along we don't know what we're trying to find.

Endless feeds put us in a perpetual state of searching, while all along we don't know what we're trying to find.

We're tired of talking about all of this because it's normalized now. Our phones are the first thing we see when we wake up and the last thing we see before we go to bed. 🌝 🌙

And yet.

Real attention is still the most important gift we can give. 🎁

So why don't we give it?

We are so desperate to avoid whatever discomfort we are experiencing in the present—an uncomfortable conversation, a difficult question, Sunday scaries—that we distract to escape our reality.

We could fill a book📚 with all the things we try to escape—but we don't have to run from them all the time. Rather, let's acknowledge their existence. Some of the negative feelings we try to escape are rooted in lies we tell ourselves about our own shortcomings.

And yet.

You are no less of a person because your clothes are piled on the floor, or you're not sure how to break your bad habits, or you can't move on from a relationship. Most people are dealing with similar challenges, but not everyone knows how to cope with them.

The things you are trying to escape don't go anywhere unless you address them or give them some room to breathe. It's perfectly safe to sit in discomfort; we just never feel like doing it.

Instead of letting negative feelings lead to escapism, allow them to lead you to self-discovery. If you want to get to know yourself, you need to get comfortable with creating silence and listen to what that person has to say to you.

Instead of letting negative feelings lead to escapism, allow them to lead you to self-discovery.

There is no downside to approaching social media mindfully. It will save you time, energy, and unnecessary guilt. You'll be challenged to deal with negative emotions in a healthy, productive way and discover "screenless joys" in the process.

Getting started is simple. Just ask yourself: *Am I being responsible with my time, or am I filtering through my apps trying to numb myself? What am I looking for?* Pause and acknowledge your own response and trust your judgment if it's telling you to look for answers in a fresh place.

Taking back control of your moments starts with noticing. Treat them as though they are precious . . .

Because they are. 😉

Broken drum

We are living the same
day over and over,
beating to a broken drum,
hearts thumping along to
the desire for things
to unfold the way we've come to prefer
over our tiny lifetimes.

We walk the streets in a
daze, telling ourselves
a story that doesn't need repeating—
rereading old messages,
searching for jobs,
and talking over each
other on the phone.

Appreciate what's right in front of you

Light pouring in streams over an
ordinary rose bush, the stranger who
asks you if you're cold without a jacket,
the jazz music floating away in the
subway station, art from a child, your
best friend's knowing laugh, a grin from
someone older who's seen more than
you and still finds a reason to look up.

Throwing coins into the proverbial
fountain is just a waste of pennies.
Could it be that a lifetime of
happy surprises is there if only
we know where to look?

It's Not the Experience—It's How You Frame It

Framing is about breaking cycles. It's a better alternative to so many fruitless endeavors—chasing happiness, searching for meaning, filling the void, regretting the past, and trying to fix suffering. With time and intention, this practice offers the structured perspective that leads to equilibrium and fulfillment.

If there's one experience in life that needs reframing, it's heartbreak. It can't be the stuff of evolution, yet my response feels almost primal. Chest constricts, breathing quickens, heart rate accelerates. Why does my body act like I'm staring at a bear when I hear a sad song at a coffee shop? 🐻☕ If I didn't know any better, I'd think I was going on coffee dates with bears. Who knew a song could trigger a fight-or-flight response?

Moving forward from heartbreak demands that we get comfortable with being uncomfortable and find healthy and effective ways to cope. My own experience taught me that the pain in my chest wasn't something I could control, but the opportunity to reframe was fully in my power. Through reflection, I began to look at my past creatively while maintaining its integrity, as if I were editing a reel of photos to see them in a new light.

If there's one experience in life that needs reframing, it's heartbreak.

I wanted to see the past through a productive lens so I could set myself free from shame, guilt, and regret. I found this

 meg grasmick

to be the ultimate form of self-care and the best road map to moving forward. There was no need to allow myself to regret what I couldn't control.

Upon sharing this perspective in my circle, a friend introduced me to Stoicism, a philosophy established by Roman Emperor Marcus Aurelius in the second century. This philosopher's top priority was to lead a virtuous life and maintain an orderly soul. He believed the only obligation you have is to yourself. Most importantly, he sought to control the things he could and forget about the rest. This simple shift in mindset was a game changer for me, and I believe it can make a significant difference for you too.

So interrupt the story you tell yourself about the past and accept when things are out of your control. Let go of ideal outcomes and focus on making choices that align with your principles. You will be filled with a deep sense of pride and the resilience to weather whatever life throws at you. There is no greater satisfaction than to be at peace with yourself, and with a commitment to that goal, you'll continue to seek and find golden truths to staying grounded.

Mirror manifesto

Life is an epic, fleeting opportunity
to learn about myself and where my
power lies. A chance to be introspective
and curious about how my mind
works without judgment or fear

I will be mindful of my blessings,
marvel at how they came to me, and be
grateful for whatever is in front of me.
I will always strive to recognize when
my efforts are "enough." Perfection
exists only in the imagination

Everything that happens is a part
of my ironing will, my opening
heart, the stretching of my

mind, and the tempering of my
emotions and expectations

I commit to this training
for the rest of my life

It's time to fall into the fulfillment
that envies my attention. To keep
pushing when the pain and bad
luck and low feelings come, as they
always do, because I know there's
something brighter on the other end

I will experience loss, I will be hurt, I
will be confused and disappointed—
and worst of all in myself. It gives and
takes. I don't know how the universe
operates or why it is here. But I will not
only search for meaning; I will create it

I will be a collaborator in the
design of my life, but I don't have
the final say in the elements that
make it a living work of art

This canvas is a gift. I don't know what
the final product will be or how much
the earth will bid; I'm only an artist
fumbling for a way to share my heart
and expose the beauty and ugliness
splashed across vibrant years

I lay down strokes with an idea, and
then a vision—a vision and then this
inexplicable, untamable thing I chase
in my dreams . . . a wild desperation
to become the art I create

And the only time to create it is now.

    IT'S NOT THE EXPERIENCE–IT'S HOW YOU FRAME IT

You Are Always in a Relationship with Yourself

When you begin mastering the art of framing, you will stumble upon a solace that can only be found through learning to trust your own mind and spirit. This process is key to nurturing a healthy relationship with yourself, one that is immovably strong and safer than any other type of commitment.

Dating in our twenties and thirties, everything is simultaneously crucial and casual. We dance between singleness, commitment, and casual dating, often ambiguous about what we really want. Discouraged by circumstance, we wait for something to work out while wrestling with questions whose answers keep slipping away. *What does my future hold? Does it even matter?*

In case this existential roller-coaster📈 isn't bad enough, we reach new abysmal lows seeing relationships advertised almost everywhere we go. Even well-meaning friends promote their happy-in-a-committed-relationship content without fully knowing their audience. So many are not in the right headspace to consume it. We love you, but all the single ladies are tired. 😴

Seeing something we wish we hadn't on social media is nobody's fault; it's just the nature of the game. Instead of giving into the trigger of coffee bears, we can view it as just another opportunity to discover the power of framing.

I've learned something very important through seasons of singleness: *You lack nothing because you are always in a rela-tionship with yourself.* 🖤🥰 It's a beautiful thing to realize. All we need to do is bolster our sense of self and be confident in our journeys.

Operating from a perceived place of lack perpetuates the feeling of emptiness. The healthiest approach to that raw feeling is to identify what prompted it: *How can I address the pit in my stomach?*

What message should I remind myself of . . .
What friend should I reach out to . . .
What book, video, or podcast can I consume . . .
. . . that will bring me to a state of equilibrium?

I used to feel like I needed to be taken care of, but now I look back and see a different person than who I am today. I'm extraordinarily grateful to have grown into a woman who is disinterested in needing, and obsessed with being all that I need. A friend of mine gave me the greatest gift when they said, "Why are you always so worried about someone taking care of you? Take care of yourself. Stand on your own two feet." 👣 To tell you the truth, I don't even recognize that girl.

In past relationships, I've made the mistake of falling for the feeling of security, but it's a dead end. By obsessing over this phantom ideal, I acted out of fear and not love and focused on all the wrong things. Security is imaginary. It's based on the idea that nothing changes and there are external forces at work that are unfailingly dependable. The illusion of security is not reliable, but independence is.

Independence is empowering.  By embracing it, you preserve your identity, values, and interests. Independence gives you permission to take care of yourself, and nine out of ten times you know best what you need.

What makes any relationship worth it is the work you put in, whether you're working on yourself or building a life with someone else.

Focusing on self-reliance is the best way to make use of seasons of singleness. The work you put in for yourself now will enable you to stick to your values, set boundaries, and establish what is imperative for you in a partner.

What makes any relationship worth it is the work you put in, whether you're working on yourself or building a life with someone else.

Either way, every day . . .

Choose you. 🙏

I choose me

Sometimes the you whom I once knew
visits me in dreams like an angel
He has your smooth skin, your
breathy laugh, your gentle touch
In fact, when I'm sleeping it's as
if you haven't changed at all

But when the morning wakes me
abruptly, as it always does,
I know I must unravel the fantasy
Like the last vacation we never took
or the vows we never wrote
Because I know we're further apart than
even the distance that separates us

Somehow that love and grief
coexist within my soul

Fumbling like heavyweight
wrestlers on the mat
Each intent on the other's destruction

And when I hear an iteration
of love gone awry, I clutch the
fabric around my chest
Push what I'm doing aside
And let myself inside the pain that
asks for my acknowledgement

But darling, I'm older now
And if only you too could see the ways
I surprise myself
With my strength and
newfound zest for life
The kind I had with your pancakes
and laundry and younger brother
You'd take a step back and say,
"That's the girl I love"

But of course, that too is a
departure from reality
A perpetuation of a fantasy
That has expired

But somewhere in one of
the four chambers of my heart
A part of me that is so terribly
young and innocent
Cries softly, and says with a small voice:
"If things were different, it
would still be you"

But things are what they are and
it's not so bad anymore
I almost laugh at the absurdity
of all that endurance
Which now feels as
easy as my disbelief

I'm truly excited to be all that I need
And learn what that means
more every day

Each miracle of a morning, I choose
to become and keep becoming
The person I love
Who loves me in return.

Gratitude Is Not Inherent—It's Learned

A healthy relationship with yourself and the world starts with gratitude; it's the number one ingredient you need to lead a fulfilling life. It takes a lifetime of trial and error to learn how to practice self-love and maintain a sense of gratitude, but the rewards are tremendous.

While we were growing up, those of us fortunate enough to have good parents went through life unaware of the sacrifices they made for our good. Gratitude is not inherent; it is taught and learned as we get older. Our immediate response to not getting our way used to be a tantrum or an acute sense that we were not being treated fairly. Eventually, it became clear that embracing gratitude was the only way to embody positivity and lead a fulfilling life.

Even as adults, it's not easy to train ourselves to be grateful in all circumstances.
Often, it goes against every fiber of our
being. We were programmed to believe
the grass is always greener, and we carry
this baggage around, even when past experience has shown us that it's a trap.
We just find new ways to perpetuate the
narrative as an excuse to be complacent
or convinced that if we don't have XYZ, we
will continue to be in a state of lack.

**Gratitude can be a
survival mechanism for
the soul and a tool to sharpen
our senses to unexpected joys.**

We may believe life will never be as beautiful as it was with our first love, or we

can't be happy until we land our dream job, or the ultimate answer to our problems is to move to the beach. Here's the truth—there *is* no such thing as an answer! When we choose to believe these random ideas about why we're not happy, we are only hurting ourselves. There is no objective truth about whether our best years are ten years in the past or ten in the future—we get to decide that through the power of framing.

Gratitude can be a survival mechanism for the soul and a tool to sharpen our senses toward unexpected joys. It turns ordinary moments into extraordinary treasures and allows us to see the people in our lives as the greatest gift of all. How would our lives change if we were to believe there is nothing better than the present moment?

It's funny how we get caught up in waiting for the external world to deliver something better than what we have in front of us. We can work hard to attract the things we want, but waiting for happiness keeps us from acknowledging the joy that is in our lap. By seeking to create wholeness within ourselves, we'll come across happy moments habitually.

The things we are waiting for don't exist. So stay hungry, but don't wait for joy.

It's already here.

Safe to swim

I will not squander the gift of life
Given by what tender

missionaries preach
And weathered monks breathe
For the illusion that I am
not exactly on the right path
Being guided by a powerfully

intimate universe

Capable of all I am not.
After every door I step through,
every year of puzzles and pain
I am closer and deeper and
more intensely conscious
of all the moments
That are leading me to discovery

I feel safest in the boat, but either way
I am floating down a river
So I'll let go of the raft,
swim with my feet up,
and try not to frown at the sun

Bewildered by possibility, enticed by
freedom, longing for security . . .
But blissfully okay with the moment.

     GRATITUDE IS NOT INHERENT—IT'S LEARNED

Heartbreak Is Not How the Story Ends

It's difficult to be grateful and live in the present when pain makes you want to escape it. As I'm writing this, I tell my mom, "I'm in a chapter where I have to be optimistic about heartbreak, and I don't know how to do it." She is laughing with me right now while she's making coffee. ☕😂 "Just be honest," she says. (Thank God there are no coffee bears in my mom's kitchen.)

I'll take her advice and be honest. There are times when I operate from a place of lack and want to throw my feelings out the window. But there are other times when pushing through moments of weakness makes me so intensely proud that I become motivated to work on myself even harder. More ruthlessly.

I push through my weakness. When it's late at night and no one's up, I identify what I

 meg grasmick

need to do to get in a better headspace. I take a breath, get off my phone, and just do it. It helps. This strength-building makes me even more grateful for the times when someone is there when I need them.

We all need emotional connections to sustain us, and the people in our circle play a vital role in filling our minds with new ideas that calm and quiet our personal narrative. And during moments when no one is there and the pain is setting in, heartbreak is as worthwhile as we can frame it. All we can do is dance in the storm, laugh at ourselves, and surrender to whatever is going on right now.

I have a friend that always says, "You never know what the tide will bring in tomorrow" (paraphrasing *Cast Away*). Life has surprised us a thousand times, and even when we underestimate the possibilities of the future, they never fail to become clear.

Often what surprises us most is our own strength in the midst of heartbreak as we wait for an easier chapter to replace our present suffering. No matter its cause, we carry on with courage.

Resilient

I lost my rock and my feet

from the same event

After stepping off the moon

Gaslighted by gravity

Swallowed by love in reverse

But in the hardest nights I was becoming

In the silent morning I was rising

In my resilient heart

Grew a fortitude that illuminated

This needed to happen

The pain was a gift

I wouldn't trade it for the world

Not for a million dollars

Not even for things to go back

to the way they were before

So thank you
For throwing magic on my weakness
And turning me into a
woman I'm proud of
For her unwavering spirit when the
odds were stacked against her

I didn't know someone could
turn heartbreak into a thing
to wonder at over coffee
Like it wasn't once poison
Until I became somebody that did.

All Shall Be Well in Time

I want to call attention to the era in which this book was born: 2020. I'm writing in the spirit of hope, courage, and resilience because they are difficult to muster. 💙 Whatever we're going through in our personal lives, from relationship hurdles to mental health issues (or far worse), everything is ten times harder.

Our challenges are magnified because the planet is beating irregularly, and it's throwing off our homeostasis. 🌎 The world is suffering from not only illness but collective emotional and economic hardship. Yet 2020 is the best example I can imagine to illustrate this simple truth: All shall be well in time. Until then, we're not in this fight alone.

It's impossible to make it through an all-time low in isolation. Loneliness was already an epidemic long before the pandemic. I experienced it myself moving to a new city and learned to lean on support like we all must, especially now. Despite our current restrictions, we are banding together more powerfully than ever.

By telling our minds beautiful stories that reframe the lie that all is lost, heartbreak will never be how the story ends.

In a moment when hearts are shrouded with pain and fear, when no one can define what normal is or predict the timeline for returning to it—even in this seemingly impossible environment—we're driven onward with faith that the best is yet to come. Everywhere there are signs of renewal, gratitude in the midst of loss, and calm amid the chaos.

Make no mistake: Nothing can stop the human spirit. We are fighters equipped with a fiery patience, as brutal and painful as it was to ignite. Our hearts beat on, and we always arise to match their perseverance.

Whatever moment we're in is an opportunity to strengthen our minds, the vehicles through which we make sense of the world. By telling them beautiful stories that reframe the lie that all is lost, heartbreak will never be how the story ends. The blissful state of okayness is always available to you in the present, no matter your circumstance.

The right path is in front of you. It's the one you've been on all along. Take it.

I'm okay

They say you wake up one day
And everything is okay
Then why do I not remember
that morning?
Was I burning the toast? Letting
the coffee get cold? Running
out without a coat?

Part of moving on is
forgetting, and part of
forgetting is moving on
All I know is that I'm changed
And even though I'm sometimes scared
to look at myself and realize I'm okay
It's the only thing that matters
Cut, stitched, and healed
I thank the universe and above all
Myself.

About the Author

Meg Grasmick has lived and breathed poetry since she was a child and loves synonyms almost as much as she hates writer's block. She moved to Santa Barbara, CA for college, where she fell in love with boba tea, coastal road trips, and the community at Westmont College. Upon graduation, she went on to earn a Master of Science degree in Integrated Marketing at New York University. In Manhattan, Meg learned that autumn and spring in the city are a dream and standing in line at Tompkins Square Bagels on a Sunday morning is always worth the wait.

Meg has a big family on the East Coast to thank for their support, including two lovely parents, three siblings, a sister-in-law and brother-in-law, six nieces and nephews, and incredible grandparents. You can find her at meggrasmick.com and follow her @alwaysarising on Instagram.